Love Pain & Poetry

Denying the Anger that's
Bargaining with the Truth

Charles Stokes

LOVE PAIN [&] POETRY
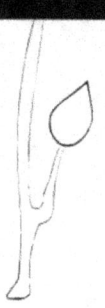

© 2018 Charles Stokes
Cover and internal design © 2018 Love, Pain & Poetry Publishing. Charles Stokes, Andre Romious
Cover Illustration: Sterlin Griffin
Interior Images: Andre Romious, Sterlin Griffin
All rights reserved. No part of this book may be used or reproduced in any manner without express written permission from the author except in the case of brief quotations embodied in critical articles and reviews.

ISBN-13: 978-1-732-1532-2-6

Reader,

This book was enhanced for your enjoyment. This is my first book where I tell the story of all that my heart has been through. It didn't meet the standards I hold for myself and the standard of subsequent books. So, I updated it with new poems to give you a better read. I really hope you enjoy the poems and poetic prose contained herein.

It's important that you know Depression effects millions of people each year. Some never disclose others have breakdowns and a number of them go on to attempt and complete actions that lead to the end of their lives.

You by being cognizant of those around you what they are going through are a first line of defense. Call your friends let them know you love them. Check on them. You never know how close you are to the next suicide. It only takes 13 seconds to decide to take your life. If you suspect a friend is suicidal call for help don't try to be a hero. If you are present and there are no dangerous weapons stay with them until help arrives don't let them out of your sight.

This book contains two suicide attempts and two other deaths. Let this serve as a trigger warning. The crux of my story also contains talk of an abortion. If those things bother you I'll name the poems here. A Drink, Your Death Killed Me and Letter to a Friend.
This book is the story of depression a real event where I record poetry saving my life. The majority of this book was written in the middle of my episode. Please practice self-care and Write For Life.

DEDICATION

I would like to dedicate this work to all the people who inspired this spontaneous moment of creativity.

CONTENTS

Acknowledgments — xi

1 LOVE

This Book	2
Bargaining with Denial	3
In a Sentence	4
Love	5
I am an ex	7
Life	8
Deep Sea	9
She Chose her fate	10
Driving Shots	11
You Spoke lies to life	12
Two Hand Touch	14
I'm Alone	15
Shattered	16
You Reap	17
Sapio Sexual	18
Always Gone	19
I Love This Woman	20

	Fight For You	21
	Haiku	22
	Quote	23
	My Love Travels Where Your Wind Blows	24
2	PAIN	27
	Quote	28
	Angel Eyes	29
	Friends	30
	'Twas you who labeled me a stalker	32
	Too Much Pride to Crash Your Homecoming	33
	Savoir	34
	Embrace it	35
	At first sight	36
	Oblivious	37
	Love comes in a Spectrum	38
	Beauty of life	39
	My Toxic Sugar	40
	Let Love Free	41
	Fall	42

Near Mars	43
Pain	44
Platform	46
Lost in it all	47
Red Roses Actually Turn Blue	48
R.E.S.I.S.T	49
Your Face	50
The Truth	51
Tantrum	52
I page	53
Your Death Killed Me	54
Letter to a Friend	55
Three Year Old Road Kill	56
To My Tears	57
Missing	58
Feeling	59
It's Been Three Long Hard Years and I Still Love You	60

3 POETRY

Summer is disrespectful	62
Spiteful	63

14 lines of doubt	64
I Was in Love Once	65
An Uneasy Apology	73
Beautiful Mind Soft hearts	74
Rich and Worthless	75
Dreaming	76
A Drink	77
I'm Over it	78
Keep Dreaming	79
Grinding my Teeth	80
Title Bout	81
EPIC	83
Fighting	91
Dear	92
Lies take too much exercise	94
Untitled	95
Index	97
Contact	100
About the Author	102

ACKNOWLEDGMENTS

I want to thank my brother Zachary for encouraging this book. Without him this book would not exist. I want to thank my parents for their support. I want to thank Cheryl Lunn and Catt Cousins for all the phone calls and advice. Most importantly I want to thank God because without him this book does not come to fruition. Finally, I want to thank everyone who purchased this book. I hope you receive the message. Write 15 minutes a day for mental hygiene.

A Note from the Author

If you really want to enjoy this book you have to read it like a... No, not like a novel. Read it like you're auditioning for a play. Like your life depends on it. Like you're getting paid to read it. Well, you are probably paying to read this book. So read it like you don't want to waste your money. If you do that you will find the true rhythm of my poetry and really get the connection you look for in works like this. The words resonate but the rhythm and rhyme get intimately close to your heart. As you read this book "correctly," you will hear my influences in rhyme. Because then and only then will I know you have truly embraced this work. This book was originally formatted for pure fun. I wanted to flip off the book industry and make this truly artistic project. But I couldn't resist the idea of having a real book. So enjoy this book like you would an aged scotch slowly and sip. The font size changes throughout this book are intentional. If there are any issues, just stop by the website and make a complaint with the author.

Racing Depression

I want to wipe away the pain

Like my mind has wiped away my gains

I don't really want to leave and walk away from my fame

Exhausted from the games I work for no reward

At work and there is a void No love No leadership or life

It's been destroyed, I walk so empty I hope my loved ones forgive me,

I can no longer take the stress I have to admit I'm a mess

I feel this is the end of the road a turn or a bend,

I simply must confess just to get this off my chest, I really need to rest

In this pursuit of happiness, I have more but I gained less,

Material items mean nothing people are amazingly wealthy, aren't they something

I'm not going to make it, not coming, I have my track shoes on I'm running,

The pen is out of ink so I'm done but the poetic bug is still humming.

LOVE

Denying The Anger [&] Bargaining With The Truth

When our seas parted
I thought we'd meet again
For our waters to mesh
Our lives to mend
and my heart would remain whole again
Not sitting is the shallow hole
My heart lives in
Reading this you'll see my hurting heart
and busted metaphors
My crippled mind and limping thoughts
My calloused hands;
hearts aching chorus
You'll see my dripping tears penned between the stanzas
and my semi depressed mind pushed its limits
You'll see writing healing me.

-this book

Charles Stokes

If I could change a thing
I'd change it all.
What I said what you did.
How far we've slid.
Wrong and happy is better
 than right and angry
bargaining with my denial

Denying The Anger [&] Bargaining With The Truth

It bothers me that my partner miss read my hand

I was holding all of her—
Her diamonds her hearts,

I told her everything, I did everything I said
but turn my cards face up
I didn't want to cheat I wanted to win straight up
and she was my dream brown skin,
light make up all natural no lace front.

-IN A SENTENCE

Charles Stokes

LOVE

It brought you into this world,
pressed and primped your hair to curl,
Anxiously gave your first of pearls,
fed you when it could not feed itself
housed and clothed the best it could on limited wealth,
Everything was sacrificed liberty and health,
for your wellbeing.

It could have just abandoned you, let you attend
school with just one shoe,
But every year managed not one but two,
I'll give you candy in the school yard,
Dry your tears when life's hard,
uplift you with my remarks,

It will wake you up in the morning,
yet when you're older stay through the night for your
enjoyment,
I will always be present after a great performance,
whether it's sports,
or success in the bed boardroom or court,

I am everything you live for,
I am rich and yet still poor,
Tangible but you can't touch,
I move yet you can't rush,

Denying The Anger [&] Bargaining With The Truth

I can be captured but never permanently plastered,
Money can't buy me, I'm a cut above the rest,

So promise me with a diamond,
Show me in your last breath..
I am known by many names, you know me as
husband daddy   mommy
I won't mention the rest, I am love you know precisely
where to find me. **Never push me to the left!**

Charles Stokes

I unwittingly helped
a robber relocate
my greatest
possession...

You

-I am an ex

Denying The Anger [&] Bargaining With The Truth

If it were up to me
I'd write you til my fingers fall off
until my chest got dry
with a scratching cough
I know our status
I don't like that loss
I'm certain you always knew
My chest aches that you're not my wife
But at one point I felt that ripe....
Struggling accepting facts
I have gripes but I guess that's...
Life

DEEP SEA

Intelligence often overlooked,
for visual stimulation,
which translates to an artificial situation,

>Depth missed,
>for shallow hits,
>particle board exchanged for solid red bricks,
>
>My insults should strike,
>like sharp stone and blunt sticks,
>Drown in her leagues,
>
>drink in her seas, choke on the ocean,
>Tremble her knees,
>Share with her peace,
>
>stroke left stroke right,
>Rest on her beach,
>Take a minute meditate deep breaths, celebrate,
>
>She oooohhh you ahhhh, She move you pause,
>the next set is your purpose and cause,
>Ride the wave respect the seas laws,
>ride her energy watch the earth pause.

Denying The Anger [&] Bargaining With The Truth

SHE CHOSE HER FATE

Love be honest with me,
I can love you and not desperately be,
Infatuated by you,
Only queens, D.R. and the bayou.

Managed to catch me by surprise,
my attention always came by the level of a drive
Often disappointed and left feeling sadly, don't give me pity,
I've seen more games than Milton and Bradley,

I'll retreat in defeat gladly,
But it was never my intent to lose your friendship,
you should have asked me, yes, I wanted to love you
not at the expense of your pretty white teeth,
Gently smiling at me beneath, that angelic disguise you call a face,

Your absence and silence left me out of place,
What you missed was that put nothing above you,

Accepted as you are,
how you come,
the game lost or won,
I wanted you around rain hail sleet snow and definitely in the sun,
Can't explain can't describe just fix it now so we're not done...

Ne-Yo said it best please be my other gun.

Charles Stokes

I was double fisted into the relationship called us
six pints in
off my stool
Drunk on love
Affixed on you
I didn't like the hangovers
I loved getting there

-DUI

Denying The Anger [&] Bargaining With The Truth

YOU SPOKE LIES TO LIFE

You spoke lies to life they still breathe
In the hearts of the ears you whispered
People falsely believe that I am a monster
you created over a warm cup of tea
and over you two I still grieve.

You smiled in my face lied to my back
Tricked me into believing my advance would bring
 a slow clap
Wedding bells rice and blessings being thrown at our backs

But you gave me sugar laced with poison,
Sent lead to target like a soldier at Chosin
as I traversed that basin full of joy
Thoughts of love stuck in my head
I got shot left for dead

In the cold on a river bank to bleed out with no bread
my heart starved for years naturally needing sugar
My body grew too weak I didn't move for days or weeks

In disbelief, love could cause—
and effect this much grief on one soul.
Lying got you nowhere the facts are written,
and the collective is now aware, of your dirty filthy underwear.

Charles Stokes

Love did prevail,
despite your disgusting attacks.
Cleverly veiled at destroying me,

I still love us,
Still love you,
and I still love the idea of we.

You spoke lies to life,
they still breathe.
You took a life,
he can't see.

Denying The Anger [&] Bargaining With The Truth

Two Hand Touch

This is football
I have many plays
I can rush or pass kick

End zones moving right pass your hips
If your hearts hands are ready to catch
What I'm throwing through your past
I'll love you forever

With no penalties in romance
Go to the locker room remove pants
I see you played the game today with no pads

Charles Stokes

The language of my love was Spanish
her second tongue French
I guess our communication mattered
it all looks shattered from my vantage

Her antics maddened me love arrested it
Poems on poles and I protested it.

It wouldn't be enough to confess to this

I just hope she knows she's not alone
It hurts and she's missed.

I just hope she knows she's not alone and it hurts

I just hope she knows she's not alone
I just hope she knows
I just hope
I just
-**I'm alone**

Denying The Anger [&] Bargaining With The Truth

SHATTERED

Far-fetched hope lead to shattered dreams

Disheveled clothing and shattered seams

Lead to lost goals and tattered jeans

Leads to thoughts of failure and silent screams

brought on by desperation and violent dreams,

I'm going to make it by any means, I'm at your front door and

I have a dream.

Charles Stokes

YOU REAP...

I find you fleeting

Too often repeated

Full of loud sound
No result
Raising your boisterous voice
But often complacently seated

You're the termite
and I am the wood
But I am still untreated
Your words sow the ground

But you forgot to seed it
So we will lack growth
We will wither
In between breaths we cry
Knowing plants need carbon
To provide life to us
We keep emitting garbage
Our plants aren't ripe!

SAPIO SEXUAL

I fell in love with your soul,
long before thinking,
of you out of your clothes.

Your mind turns me on.
The algorithms explanation, speaks more than,
the skirt you have on.

Imperfectly sprung.
Your mental and spiritual,
 have me perfectly won.

I need algebra to get back to one,
(a)equal 1 x is 3 y is the unknown. x times itself
plus 1 is we.

I know that's a bit much,
not looking for your clothes. Dating is a risky market,
I see a stock I have to close.

Let me send my offer.
Full price,
I Propose!!!

Charles Stokes

ALWAYS GONE

If home is where the heart is then my heart is never home, always dreaming up new places so my heart may roam.

My daughter keeps me leveled
but only when she's home,
when she departs my heart is always gone.

I can't replace feeling with our conversations phone,
I try to write her emails but I always miss in tone,
I'll try again tomorrow but we miss because of zones.
And it hurts,
I know she cries because daddy always gone.

Denying The Anger [&] Bargaining With The Truth

I LOVE THIS WOMAN

I love this woman like I love my mother I love this woman like I love no other,
She keeps me focused,
Nags me like seasonal locust,
Natural hair gets wet its hocus pocus,
She dress so presidential, commands my focus,
We work together like bees, I drive her lotus,
so secure, money for you rotors,
She gonna pump your brakes, maybe send you out for cold cuts,
We so wide open, Bush or Romney couldn't close us,
When we together christian and religion couldn't cloth us,
The game wide open, I provided word they call it spoken,
She's Bonnie I'm Clyde we got it smoking.
I love this woman like I love no other, I love this woman as much my mother
There is no other,
Do I cheat?, side chic is not in my speech
Let me repeat,
That woman there is my lover,
 She my mistress and my other,
She told those versions of herself I was with no other,
And when that gets old,
I was with my brother,
Disloyalty between will remain undiscovered,
Temptations is not an issue I got that covered
I love this woman as much as I love my mother,
I love this woman like I love no other....

FIGHT FOR YOU

I am only still standing here because you asked me to fight
I would have said no had I known

You'd be the opponent asking me to

Love you
Hate you
Date you
Make you
My wife

But don't ask me to fight for you
It's like asking for my life
Especially if you have no intentions on fighting me back

Without you I can never relax or get back that piece of me which speaks to me to love you It perplexes my senses

Even while your old space is newly rented
women now think I'm damaged

but it just means
I know what love is
and I don't take it for granted

Denying The Anger [&] Bargaining With The Truth

Beauty speaks to me
Like religion teaches me
love is to be shared

Haiku

Charles Stokes

Pain is inevitable in growth,
You will find that the person you become through it is worth every lie, every fail, and every no.

-Charles Stokes

Denying The Anger [&] Bargaining With The Truth

She said I didn't hold her in high regard
I declined to agree
I said

You wanted unrealistic
I gave you my time
All of it

You wanted my attention
I gave you my mind
All of it

You wanted my love
I gave you my heart
All of it

You never gave it back.
I looked in your trash out back
Not there

I looked in my closet
Not there

I checked my trunk
Still empty

I saw you you saw me
It was there
You wanted me in pain
So you kept it

No one told you I ached
Pained, died twice?

Charles Stokes

No one let you know I never wanted you to go, depart or start over?

Despite this crushing weight of the luggage you left.

You managed to secure the bag
With my heart packed in it.

I guess that's what separates us
I'd never let you cry alone
Just ask anyone who knows

My love travels where your wind blows

This page was intentionally left blank.

PAIN

Denying The Anger [&] Bargaining With The Truth

My pain tells the story of her reverence

- The truth in a sentence

                    Charles

ANGEL EYES KILLING ME

Heart Spoken

Pretty eyes

Heart throbs

Silly lies

Rob

Me of breath

Joyful sobs

Next to death

I never saw a more beautiful set of eyes
Hidden behind them cleverly hidden lies
with thick voluptuous thighs to match
Allah cleverly delivered a prize
Beautifully wrapped wearing a violet niqāb
shimmering hair and a face only fit for gods
Not only in made up face
but her heart matches the facade.

Denying The Anger [&] Bargaining With The Truth

Friends

Could never use the word,
to describe you,
you turned your back,
I was depressed, deep dark blue.

My grandfather died,
my heart ached,
no one saw tears,
I called you.

I know I was wrong for advancing,
but you missed the pain,
hidden in that embarrassing exchange,
and selfishly planted space.

I thought we were the best of,
what love could offer,
despite declining my offer,
 rejection is normal I stayed in my place

The contempt in your rebuke,
Showed what you thought of me.

It's like a house you want to view.
then the agent reduces you, to what you do.

As if I couldn't afford or,
I wasn't valuable enough to explore.

I just asked for a date, not for your drawers

Charles Stokes

God had me on this journey
showed me truth.
I just wish it was anyone but you.

Unconditional and no repent,
sincere until the end.

I found beauty in your being.
I briefly liked your Zen.
Emotionally distraught,
How could that be a sin?
I am espoused to the truth now,
YOU are not my friend.

Denying The Anger [&] Bargaining With The Truth

'TWAS YOU WHO LABELED ME A STALKER

'Twas you who labeled me a stalker

Dragged me uplifted yourself,
Conceited.

But it was you who said never give up,
I believed it.

It was you who sold your parents story,
Twice repeated.

I did just that and gave chase,
found defeat.

How'd you do my program like that,
Control, alt, delete.

I couldn't breathe.
How could you up and leave?

Drag me through the mud and dirt,
I couldn't grieve.

You seduced my heart
murdered it,

We were going to make it,
Despite our tumultuous start.

Charles Stokes

When you think I'm stalking
but I'm in New York with a newer you
in fact by that time I had a few of you
I'm not saying that I was in love or trying to screw a few,

you knocked me off a mountain
I did what most would dew,
You sent shade shadowed in hate
I sent love in multitudes

You kept dastardly dragging, blatantly bashing, talking exerting energy

I couldn't combat the lies

Slashing and thrashing
Stabbing and jabbing

I was busy exerting my energy
two hundred miles away.
I was with the woman I expected you to become.

-too much pride to crash your homecoming

Denying The Anger [&] Bargaining With The Truth

SAVIOR

    I **walked** into a cross roads,
    I kept walking until
    that intersected with a lost road.

    I stopped to ponder,
    What should be my fate,
    Two miles in each direction wandered,
    I can be anything but late.

    A woman crossed the path,
    I enjoyed as suns past, two weeks ago today,
    Will make the last her shadow cast, I remember well,
    She walked silently to my past.

    Another crossed the path
    quickly discarded bags
    she spent many nights
    Uplifting as spirit dragged
    Protecting me from the last

    She escorted me to our future,
    ages from my heavy bags.

    On our new road,
    She lightened my life, reduced my heavy loads.
    She was the cross in my road.

Charles Stokes

EMBRACE IT

People run from love because it's not coming,

from where they think it should,

When love comes it's usually free and not always,

exclusively romantic

You ask, how could this be?

Love is a living thing it grows and withers,

If you kill it?

It will return weak sickly and timid.

When you run from love,

You leave space for hawks, chickens, and pigeons, beware of the doves

With the face of an angel, heart of a thug,
a well-dressed pigeon, designed to trick shallow hearts into poor decisions, so it can selfishly give itself.
A fresh start.

AT FIRST SIGHT

The first time I saw you black boots, brown dress, curls
looking a neat mess
never thought I'd caress the ambitious curves made
obvious by your unassuming dress

I loved you at first sight
something I've confessed
But after many years that neat appearance
is internally a compelling mess

We made passionate love for ten minutes
then immediately ejecting a mess
As you said my name I guess;
That was the best ten minutes in life
and the most memorable mess I've left

You touched my soul
lifted it right out my chest
I've repented now and laid
that part of me to rest

Charles Stokes

As the piano lays
I lay in wait
For the day to come
Where I see you run

I see your smile I've been missing for a while and in your face I see the pain of my missing child.

I've been holding it for a while my concerning discernment for mental impairment andandre denial caused by loss of a fetus I didn't protect. It only took the right words. I couldn't find them. You gave time then in a flash he was gone I found it blinding. I own the guilt. Because it's your heart I wasn't minding...

-oblivious

Love Comes in a Spectrum

How can love,
Exist as shade?

When it possesses all color grades

Love isn't void of light
It shines rays,

Love can't be black and white,

They are opposite and yet the same.

Charles Stokes

Beauty of Life

If beauty resides in the eye of the beholder,

How does death live in the eye of a soldier,
What's each breath worth as we get older,
Don't chose beauty if her heart's colder,

But don't let yesterday failures fill life with sorrows,
until you get through today and tomorrow,
love like your life depends on it
You're going to sin so repent from it

Face rejection like a champion
love her anyway like it was meant,
even when it can't be done,
that's the only way to find the one.

Denying The Anger [&] Bargaining With The Truth

My Toxic Sugar

There's no pain anymore
just burgeoning
sorrow
 deep regret
Tears of fears
Drowned in years of upset
What's left?

My conflicting emotion
Drowns in peril
Evidence washed away
spiraling tears
 sterile
like dental drills

Reaching in the cavity of my chest
Screeching scathing shrills
Discovering the darkness her departure left

If only we could undue the rotting caused by sweet cake
I could love again devouring your sweet taste

    Burrowing through my roots peering past the semblance
    of my face

Hiding my inner youth, innocence I saved for you.

Let Love Free

Love is free it's not a slave or something you cage
It's harnessed and you can pull the reigns
If you pull too hard you will never recover the gains
Even so it can still fly away

so naturally as humans we trap what we cannot tame
Behavior I frequently associate with a lame
And yet I find it so successful
Selfish only concerned to trap love in a cage

They are cancers
They impregnate
Fiscally dominate
Mentally subjugate

Love into submission and while love is there love is absent
 and mentally distracted
So that it may serve its sentence like a prisoner on death row
Realizes his existence but lack of ability to grow
Here now and in the future, trapped love ain't real love.

It's an enigma that the caged, never figure out.
The riddle the enslaver can't go without.
Love should be free anything less is slaved.

Denying The Anger [&] Bargaining With The Truth

Fall

As the leaves fell our weather cooled
kids returned to school I prepared for winter

as our leaves fell
I purchased new winter boots
for the trek I expected
your harshness would reflect

as the leaves fell
your disdain for my ruminations
made obvious by your piercing points
you stressed caressed and pressed them into my chest

as your leaves fell
I retreated to your tells you could not hide
and I no longer confide in you

as the leaves fell
our tree died you couldn't tell my mind
captured by your spell

of destructive dysfunction delusional dismissal and against all objections

as my leaves fell
I plead guilty to climbing in the passenger seat for the ride
as I stand and affirm I've been tried

Charles Stokes

Summer turned you away
From love in a pitch black inferno
of a dying star

-near mars

Denying The Anger [&] Bargaining With The Truth

PAIN

I know great pain,
the kind that gets stains in the wood grain.
I know pain like a father who lost his kids,
a man with an unfaithful wife
a man who has lost everything in life twice,
but like job I've yet to yell Christ,

I hurt like a survivor of Germany in 42,
I walk life with nothing to lose,
I got options like don't win and you lose,
I got more than a scar; click, I got proofs

Living in this vivid pain since my youth.
Love me or hate me you gotta' choose
Makes me very little difference,
I said I got nothing to lose, nothing to prove,

I got nothing for you,
So, if you gonna' love me paint the picture,
Oil and water never goes smooth,
Hopeless in romance I believe in fiction,
That's why when I look up
your arms always missing
It's another man kissing.
I was never tripping my concerns are non-fiction,

You need to part mountains, you need a little friction,
I'm cold like the Rockies,
Course, my hearts not skipping

Charles Stokes

My feelings aren't flipping
Do you need me to read it again?
I really need you to listen…

Denying The Anger [&] Bargaining With The Truth

PLATFORM

I'm sitting on the train platform,

And the clock is ticking
Red All-star flats on,
Wondering if she'll text before making a move,
Fitted worn backwards
Jeans, belt but
wish I had slacks on

Impatient at van ness
crazy how she played it
Probably took Xanax
whatever game she changed it

I know she need to text before
I lose my patience, heartbeat to a bruise
Committed, a mental patient
My mind rolls in circles
Was my gamble too hastened?

No, I say to myself
Should I have just waited?
My anticipation is raging,
I waited, she waited,
I kept praying, she never came...

 Contemplating what kind of game?
Got me on this platform thinking,
I am insane

Charles Stokes

I wallow in wells of guilt so deep
I've never seen the bottom
The pitch reminds me to respect love

I reach for ground but all I touch is the wall;
Of my heart and the pain traumatizes the armor I've donned.
  My cries are unheard and my priorities become survival.

Denying The Anger [&] Bargaining With The Truth

Red Roses Actually Turn Blue

God Blessed you with a dozen roses
you let them wither then you froze them

Defrosted, hung upside down
wrapped in paper
dried and slaughtered

Why the process to a lonely death
You took it all I have nothing left

Charles Stokes

I'd prefer this broken heart over never having met you.
I'd rather use spoken word to address you than not ever had the opportunity to undress you
I'd rather sit here in my blues
 than be empty of clues you exist
Your departure is an attack
So I stand strong I R.E.S.I.S.T
In a t-shirt of your words
It's your absence I lament

Denying The Anger [&] Bargaining With The Truth

The day I lost you I told someone
I can't unsee that
my best friend became pink mist
I'd never be the same

every soul that could
end my pain
never came

And those that did
couldn't see
Depression blinded me

You blamed me for this
With a foundation of falsehoods
And never looked in the mirror
At my shadow of fear
Powdered in hesitation
Creating the tears
I shedded the last three years

-your face

Charles Stokes

I still warm milk for you
Change your clothes
Watch cartoons
Tie your shoes
Practice daddy

I still dream
About you
Nick and toons
Your first word
Unlaced shoes
Actually saying mommy

I wish you were here
If only I spoke the right words
If only she felt what I said
But she didn't listen
To understand
I didn't take a firm stand
So I wish
I wasn't still dreaming about
Wishing I was your dad.

-the truth

Denying The Anger [&] Bargaining With The Truth

My love languishes on the ledge you left me
Brandishing Broken
Aiming at air
Socially succumbed
To your
Fleeting flight
Of
Dangerously in despair

Kicking the feet carelessly complacent and flailing the arms of madness
Only to realize your departure wasn't met
With the relief of freedom.

I predicted this painful aging raging disguised behind my timid eyes
Blinking unconcerned
But the tears you couldn't see
Undoubtedly burn

Tantrum

The phone call was painful
I dreaded it for ages
I thought of you my apple
Envisioned you on pages

I page

Denying The Anger [&] Bargaining With The Truth

Your Death Killed Me

Dying from pain moments of tranquility followed by chaos
one minute here and gone lifeless tears in my eyes
Needlessly explain

Why the ice will never melt alcohol will never tell speed with no seatbelt

Leading to tragedy with a mother at the wheel wheels never squealed brakes didn't feel

Control lost not the car but at the bar it cost me a sister, us a daughter, you a friend, her traumatic end

Ejected from the car was a part of my heart
not destined to die and still I contemplate why?

And with that the devil acted with precision when the car was done flipping my aunt was unharmed her brother broke an arm
my cousin close enough to huff on the exhaust...

Letter to a Friend

How can you destroy what you love removing key pieces
Leaving your world reaching I never saw the tears
Flow down your face speechless we could have cut through fear
Searching for safe space keeping you from departure

I stare at your face touching your cold hand
As I try not to hate you left and
I can't even grieve or begin to relate

My love ones won't cater my needs
Because they won't let me mourn you
Without reminding me to mourn for your wife
And I do not think it's right maybe it was paranoia setting in
But she was your glowing light

I reply to them on that harrowing night my brother,
my friends lives took a regrettable right I know that's not him
Like your lives, I cut this short or else it, like my tears, will never end.

Denying The Anger [&] Bargaining With The Truth

My imperfections loved perfectly
Incorrectly until you corrected course
Routing me down memory lane like an
aggressive driver on a rocky road but

 I survived her and the collision.
I remember waking up to lights, IV's and a new me.
She moved on forgetting we.

I thought it was over but the path of her tongue requires her to lie in the road of me forever. I know she's just saving face.

-3 year old road kill

Charles Stokes

The innocence lost in our exchange robbed me
 of what it was to be a man
These pages are my emancipating declaration
that I'll rise again from the ashes you left me

At my funeral existed no tears
No one mourned I died alive and still breathing
Persistent beat, scorned and in fear
Your light burned me the layers of peeling succumbed

-To my tears

Denying The Anger [&] Bargaining With The Truth

Heartbroken
I put it in the hands of a child
Who launched it from bridge
water won't flow under
That's why sometimes when I speak
My tongue bleeds (words)

I was hoping a friend, a love
Would show up with a pardon
With my face on a milk carton
Retuning me to loving.

-missing

Charles Stokes

Beautiful blue (scapes) is where my vivid mind took me
The numb possessed my flesh
resided beneath my skin as if a parasitic invader.

This was just a break-up
I was supposed to feel pain
But there was just empty numb
I had broken thumbs

My central nervous system didn't process anything for weeks. I couldn't sleep at night. She became the terrorist in my dreams and affectionately my enemy. It was weird. I wanted to yell and love at the same time. Hug and shun but in the meantime, I wanted to run away from this relationship like the Lusitania that it was. The water was rising the entire time and she was already lying. If you think about it, I was already dying. I hoped that time would cure that. It didn't, even though I've moved on. Love didn't and those tales she tells to fairies sting like honey bees in a field her army pollinates.

Denying The Anger [&] Bargaining With The Truth

If I could change a thing I'd change it all.
What I said what you did.
 How far we've slid.
Wrong and happy is better than right and angry
bargaining with my denial arguing with my truth

It's been three long hard years I still love you.

Spiteful

She walked into my loving heart
Planted herself sat and parked
I changed all my locks
I called the cops gave her a spark
no period as I run on she tore life apart

Denying The Anger [&] Bargaining With The Truth

14 Lines of Doubt

We became friends in that dust bowl
                        Four nights a week despite
Nasty food cooked by nasty trolls
                        I enjoyed you in my sight
The many days we shared a stroll
                        I embrace those moments in life
Upon return I lost control
                        and illusions of you a wife

I probably did us both a favor
I can see me cut and bleeding
Tempers flared on knives and razors
Drunken nights Bacardi chasing
Star struck lovers falling out of favor—
I wish what if kept the mind from racing

I Was in Love Once

She was a beautiful girl.

A beautiful spirit I still miss her sometimes. Ok, the days I forget she tried to stab dry crush and grind my heart into a fine sand, type of sometimes.

But no matter what I say there's no denying I love this girl. Even if she is an egotistical vindictive truth twisting pin head with thighs that give life living in her own little world.

My father keeps saying I'm glad you're over that now. I keep reminding him I will never be over that. This is love and that doesn't just evaporate into thin air because another girl comes along with fresh hair. Love is forever.

I met her bowling on my brother's birthday. Now she had on these ripped up jeans that her thighs were busting out of that could barely contain

"THAT ASS"

I mean you have to know she jumped wiggled and cartwheeled herself into these jeans she knew what she was doing. And she shook

"THAT ASS"

every time she knocked down pins.
So naturally just moving from Hawaii not seeing any sisters for 6.2 years I'm sorry I called texted and did whatever I had to do for her attentive ears.

Denying The Anger [&] Bargaining With The Truth

I know what you're thinking. You're wrong, the night we met I took her home and we had this conversation and I thought it was pretty deep even though putting a kiddie pool out on the lawn with my favorite beer in summer is depth.

It's just like getting what you want from the water without all the formalities of registration, paying, rules, you know a lifeguard barking orders and sharks.

So finally she and I go on a date I was in love with

"THAT ASS"

so all she had to do was not be crazy. So we end up in my car kissing, and low and behold no sex was given...

As I drive home cursing and shit! I'm thinking damn, no matter what she does from now I'm not going to want to think she's a hoe. Man logic we really ain't that smart when faced with mesmerizing decisions like

"THAT ASS"

Luckily while she is all the things I stated above.
I don't think she's a hoe to this day. But I lost that important chess game that most don't know they play.

She checkmated me a week before May. So two weeks in I get a knock at the door. It's an ex, a Dominican ex that I haven't seen in a year. She comes in and I'm thinking "That ass".

(Reference "At first sight")

But the weird thing is I don't want any of

"THAT ASS."

So I tell her about my girlfriend. I feed her and before the day is out I have a hole in my door from a wine bottle I drank the night before. So naturally I kick her ass out and I call my girlfriend up like hey... Now mind you two weeks in I'm thinking I have two more weeks to clean out my "Trash".

You know get rid of all...

"THAT ASS"

So I begin to tell her what happened. By the end of the week, the message of hole in door got leaked. It became destroyed the apartment as it was relayed to me from my brother...

So I guess you're wondering why my brother is telling me the apartment was destroyed.

Well my future sister in law...

...is this girl's best friend.

This was the first alarm.
                The exaggerated events.

Anyway, I didn't think anything of it at the time. But for all the trouble. I should have gotten

Denying The Anger [&] Bargaining With The Truth

"THAT ASS"

from the Dominican one last time.
I know you guys are thinking "WHY"......

I went a whole damn week without

"THAT ASS"

for telling the damn truth.
But we made up 8 days later

So anyway time passes. I notice something really fucking awkward like pauses in the middle of conversations. To me that means it's my turn to talk. I literally have 4 thoughts go through my head between speech. It was agonizing to me to her I was being rude. Look 4 seconds is all you get in a conversation between sentences, not 10 minutes leaving my mind to wonder. What she was doing was calculating, so it left me to ponder? What takes ten minutes to calculate?

"THAT ASS"

So anyway I get a weird feeling after a heated discussion in Chinatown while riding the red line. I wanted to break up with her right there on the platform. We kept arguing over the smallest shit but it got back to me through my brother as a big huge issue. So she begs me not too. All I can think of is

"THAT ASS"

Ok, I'm lying she was really pretty and smart too.

So, fast forward a little bit... it's my birthday and I'm turning 35.

    I didn't even think anything of the milestone. This girl takes me to see D.C. Jazz festival, legal sea foods and I got my haircut and a facial at Michaels I think that's what it's called. The biggest surprise was she secretly invited my brother and future sister in law to dinner. The girl stole my heart. She was definitely a winner.

D.C. Jazz festival.

Its summertime, it's muggy so I ask are we gonna' be inside or what. She never says... so I'm sweating like shit think of a word rhymes with buck in my GUCCI. So instead of getting upset I began joking. Comes off as completely unappreciative. Got it my bad I'm sorry. She could have answered my inquiry.

I mean if I would have had her out there hot and bothered we would still be together just so she could torment

> "MY ASS"

as I am doing her right now. Satan was in town as that sweat rolled down my back, like a hand crank window. Real creepy real slow.

But I felt like a Slave
    on the Potomac in winter clothes

Denying The Anger [&] Bargaining With The Truth

> *putting coal in a furnace who hadn't had a sip of water in three days.*
> *I mean I was hot enough for three slaves.*

I was like Jeffery with an ascot equipped silver trays,
dressed for Sunday worship and praise,
with the air out, fans broke
it's so hot in the pew your leg flairs out
just to get some air, ladies you know what I'm talking about because your hair wears out.

I needed a damn distraction!!!!

                        Jokes "R" US I became...

if I could have made a goat laugh I would have tried it.

So anyway fast forward we're leaving legal seafood

in an UBER and I've had a great time, I'm grateful very grateful but the libations are taking effect and I'm still joking and laughing getting those birthday vibrations. But this poor girl feels under attack so we get to her place. I can't remember what we ended up arguing over but it was probably silly and I ended up not getting

         "THAT ASS."

Oh, that's it, I didn't want to sleep on a sheet less mattress.

So I found myself out on

         "THAT ASS."

But what I left out was midway through the day.

Charles Stokes

I realized I was going to marry

"THAT ASS."

Yeah right Spoke Karma... Two weeks later she'd find out she was pregnant I'm not sure if this is relevant. Even though I hesitated, as she asked about the baby, Deep down in my heart I really want the lady.

   But her exaggerations really kept me from engaging.
   Trying to find my needs,
   Her delicate emotions raging,
   my conscious told me take heed.
   But not that it would be detrimental to my seed,
   Take my three hearts pack up and leave with no reprieve

   Two weeks after that we'd break up.....
   A day after meeting my parents

I pleaded and pled for her not to leave,
I put it all out there
Wore it on my sleeve,
I cried and I tried,
I really want to believe,
That's she would at all cost protect that seed.

I bought a calligraphy pen,
I made that pen bleed,
I wrote sloppy and the same thing on repeat,
Depression was setting in and I couldn't sleep,
How could I lose this thoughtful girl?
How could she not see?

Denying The Anger [&] Bargaining With The Truth

That her exaggerations were trying,
and I couldn't get past it,
How I was at home with her.
Parisian and plastered.
My mother didn't raise me to raise bastards.
I loved no I love this girl... she was a classic.

The whole time I'm fighting for my heart,
This girl is ripping me apart

to whoever would listen...

Time heals all wounds
Don't flex the stitching to soon,
Give it til' half past noon.
　It's like new now, Seal the heart up,
　These women will run it down with light trucks

Walk around

Walk away not giving two fucks...

She responds to how she feels. Not the truth, so I'm not sure if that's lying is it? I guess we all have to determine what it means to each of us....

If you want to know what happens during the break up and what I think of her to this day read the Depression & Its Acceptance.

Charles Stokes

An Uneasy Apology

I've held close how I made you cry
I accept responsibility so I try
I keep record of when you've cut your eye

I miss your joy
I can't get past your missing voice
I'm stuck having to repair that tie
I survived repeating your lie

Subconsciously, I made the decision
as ridiculous as I was I never envisioned
that your revenge would be mostly my decision
what's transpired was not the vision

So now I toil over why you no longer listen
I'm a love felon serving a sentence
I've scorned the warden
I'm desperate for parole here's my repentance

I lied to self about what I envisioned there's
not a time I imagined you outside my decisions
You have my heart our love my religion.

I'd Jordan or spark about town with no cares
but my legs and lungs are weak with no heirs.

Denying The Anger [&] Bargaining With The Truth

Beautiful Mind Soft Hearts

> The most beautiful part of your body
> is where it's headed
> Your mindless journey
> is where it parted,
> grew legs and walked off
> on the way it got sick,
> from the frost
> and stopped to cough
>
> Your arms brought you back
> when you were once lost it all cost
> merely time and a harder journey
> one we both lost
> but this is what makes you so beautiful
> and my heart soft.

Rich and Worthless

You asked for a second chance
and are given a mouth to empty out of
It was always about you
and never about love

Always about money and rarely about hugs
then I realized the danger that is you
so I let go

At first my absence you will not know
it will be tranquil as if undisturbed snow
as the clock ticks, snow melts
my conspicuous absence deeply felt

The fountain I used to be will be frozen,
Early March—
 mark my word, my love will not flow.

Denying The Anger [&] Bargaining With The Truth

Dreaming

First sight of you made me smile
walking as we talk I admired your smile
That day we walked a block,
I focused on the mile

I really had something for you
Life had something else in mind
You presented opportunity
I was blindly involved in mine

Regretting hasty action
Which seemed wise at the time
Beautiful black queen
You're still seen in my dreams
      a prize at this time

I'd love to—
But my next line
Our reality
Doesn't rhyme with mine.

A Drink

The ink bleeds into my silver sink,
I should call the ambulance, as I wait I pour a drink,
I mix hot sauce with vodka, in a tall glass as
I spill it in the sink.

The medic shows he grabs my coat—
 the mink.
My neighbor is an activist the satisfaction in his wink,
standing with his bucket firm brimming with fake ink.

I submit this gory form, to God
 I in my British Voice;
This is what I bloody think.

Hands me back my gory paper
 re-fills my pen with ink,
the medic thanks me for the caper
Hail to Mary clean the Bloody sink.

Denying The Anger [&] Bargaining With The Truth

I'M OVER IT

I'm over it—
It's funny how people use you, stab you in the chest,
leave you to bleed, straight through the vest, it covers the phone,
text after text, you bleed for reset, trust,
love, invest,
there's nothing left, the love is real,
you're left a teary mess, I'm over it...
you go hard, til the love stops...til the heart pops
and the pain rests, and the texts stop,

I'm over it—

But like a slain friend,
the feeling stays familiar, repeat the situation,
the tingling peculiar, she ain't Heidi,
that won't seal, not slightly, leaking love,
You weep I feel, get over it,

But eventually you realize it's not them,
you love too hard, and trust too much,
you're too material, not cute enough

she don't like the way you sleep, eat, snore,
bore her pistons to the core, wishing you would creep,
So she would have a reason, to find elsewhere to sleep

Get over it

That shit your mother taught you

is not good enough,
you become selfish, bad boy,
you on a mission for bad toys,
what makes her any different?

I'm just a cold dude given cold cards,
it make me so rude,
I got too much going on for emotional scars,
So I...get over it.

I'm married to the money,
I like to stack my G's I got no real time for honey's
I like my q's but I love my p's
I'll dot those eyes and cross those t's
working on a recipe, in the kitchen,

Constantly, stuffing my face,
never pause for a 10, or queen, only an Ace,
seek yourself a trophy, you'll find few
that fit in a case...

I'M OVER IT

Denying The Anger [&] Bargaining With The Truth

Keep Dreaming

The scars and age that a hard life leaves,
I can see the beauty that you once possessed
Kid or two drugs took what you had left
Coupled with the alcohol a disaster in itself
If you only had another chance you could be someone else
Put your old life on a shelf.
I can see you dreaming had you grown up somewhere else

You can stop dreaming now
You can make it real
Focus on the dream and follow what you feel
Harness all that pain I can see that shit can kill
And reach out for those dreams like you used to reach for Pills.

Charles Stokes

There's no pain anymore
Just burgeoning sorrow
 deep regret—

Tears of fears
Drowned in years of upset
What's left?

My conflicting emotion drowns in peril
Evidence washed away spiraling tears
 sterile like dental drills

Reaching in the cavity of my chest
Screeching scathing shrills
Discovering the darkness
Her departure left

If only we could undue the rotting caused by sweet cake
I could love again devouring your sweet taste

Burrowing through my roots
peering past the semblance of my face
Hiding my inner youth
Innocence I saved for you

-grinding my teeth

Denying The Anger [&] Bargaining With The Truth

My heart aches
 stalled fakes
Pretending to want love and misty eyed fights
The kind where no one launches heavy handed rights

But descriptive verbs
That land below the belt
Still blacking eyes
That see you as their heirs prize
crawling back from destruction

A feat many won't do they simply haven't the tools or instruction

Block, keep punching.

-Title bout

Epic

I.

She struggles with mental health,
Struggles with simple tasks
Like paying things sometimes
And keeping food on the shelf,

You tell her she ain't together,
But the one thing she gets right is you,
The one thing she's on time with is you,
That's the one thing she does well,
Be glad the other isn't you,

Uplift her for in her anxiety,
She's still brilliant,
Fun, loving and vibrant.
With you she's less empty
And sometimes even thriving,

She ignores your exasperated demands,
That she get more hands
Or to write things down as if
she's gone mad
It simply can't be that bad
And what's wrong with yours?

Denying The Anger [&] Bargaining With The Truth

II.

That is her normal and her
Formally notifying you
That is if you can't love her at her worst
Then your relationship rests peacefully in a hearse

So while you are complaining
of her sporadic behavior,
She manages to wash your clothes,
and feed your children,
She manages to hear needs and often fills them.

And while she needs you to pick up the pieces,
You miss the cues and sleep on the floor,
where she often leaves them
as she listens at the door,
For you to come rescue her from mental demons,

Charles Stokes

III.

She covers you sleeping
Sits and listens to your heavy breathing,
prays to God and talks to you,
While praying you are receiving.

She prays real hard hoping, swearing,
that you or God will hear her mental tearing
She's tired of keeping children and mental bearing, she needs a break
But thinks you're not caring

So at the kitchen she's staring,
It's a mess you left some pieces,
You left your fork knife and plate,
and Reese's pieces.

The dishes because she preps your meals,
So instead of wash them you had your fill,
played with kids, called up bill,
Snuck upstairs to get some kills.

While you played games she,
Ironed your shirt.
Pulled your shoes out for work,
Thought about that lingerie
She'd scantily wear for you and twerk,

Problem is your epitomized as a dick
Unequivocally a jerk,
and years in you've kept your ears in
your rears end.

So there's a couple wrinkles in your shirt.

Denying The Anger [&] Bargaining With The Truth

IV.

As you sleep as a baby, as she has three of them,
the oldest requires the most care,
and again she covers him.

She goes to clean up his silly mess,
Moving the tear soaked pillow from her chest,
Stepping over as if husband of the year,
You know best.

Would rant and rave ignoring his own mess,
To again get the messy house off his chest,
She picks a plate and grabs fork,
Washing dishes thinking pork,
She pulls it out to thaw,
Washes hands grabs a pot,
Begins to wash and stares again
at the ticking clock,
Looks down to grab another dish,
Saw a blood soaked crock—

The knife you left cut her wrist,
As left in a soap suds pot,
She made a screeching scream,
And hit the floor and panicked,
Grabbed the dish towel
Trying to make the flow stop,
As it was only slightly canted,
That vein was fully popped.

Charles Stokes

V.

As you awoke to find your love,
Bleeding out on the floor she loved,
You in a panic you called your parents,
Left the kids fast asleep
peacefully in their beds.
You're so sporadic and driving faster
save the woman from being dead.

In your mind she committed suicide
So you slow the ride,
but how would you look in your kids eyes,
If you let mommy die?

You pressed the gas
Touched the clutch,
and now the car is moving fast.

You reach the hospital
Almost crash,
You grab you wife
Stain the dash.
She's bleeding out,
Her pulse is weak
The doctor asks all he can.

Denying The Anger [&] Bargaining With The Truth

VI.

But she can barely speak
They get the gurney put her on,
Roll her back flashing through your past
you noticed she has your sweater on,

And all you do is gasp,
How could you be so unconcerned,
With that woman you don't deserve,
Who raised your kids,
And never curved,
Your advances to other words,
From lessor men who at least would
have appreciated her.

As you sulk her parents come,
Your face is blank,
you commune as one,
Racing thoughts of being done,
this crazy woman raised my son.

Left and right your mind confused,
How did you miss all the cues,
Ego too large to blame yourself,
Put your pride aside
and love the one whom you confide,
This has been a bloody ride.

It's all too much for you to bare,
They call a cart they call the crash,
You pray to god please save my ass.
I have been an awesome dad.

VII.

Epiphany comes as god responds:

You've been ignoring her weeks.
I love my child she's anointed,
You horrible husband and yet favored
You keep my child disappointed,
I want her home for reassurance
You judge unfairly
She doesn't
deserve your annoyance.

She is a gift
I want her back,
Your own rib but
You don't have her back.
The doctor comes
he shakes his head
you cry you wait
you know she's dead,

The guilt it trips
what-will-you-tell-the-kids?

The doctor says she's stable breathing,
but they briefly lost her on the table,

Cognitive function limited,
Her body isn't able...

He asks about advance directives
her parents study your subjective,

Denying The Anger [&] Bargaining With The Truth

Thoughts and faces,
hoping you love their daughter
as much as you've projected...

The doctor leaves he shuts the door
her parents fall both to floor
You're sick you vomit, mind won't endure,
What you've been dealt, body shakes its core.

Fighting

Depression steals your heart
like an unengaged wife
dampers your perception
of what should be god given rights

I'm not trying to be the tough guy I am usually
because life gave me a black eye where my ego used to
be

I'm still fighting to get used to me
you have no idea what that would mean and
I can't imagine the guy they are used to seeing.
I'm not crazy just hurt from trying to be a good human
being.

Denying The Anger [&] Bargaining With The Truth

Dear...

Two years have elapsed and any dreams I once had of having you back all but collapsed into a river of aggressive water that slaughters men entering its guarded borders.

Because I've shared history people think I'm broken but it's likely I'm outspoken but a man as resilient as I will remain unbroken and while I've done a lot of coping. I rest easy knowing that despite my flaws. My reality wasn't lost. This book exists only because I found love. I realize that no matter how much you go through it. Preparation and anticipation will not help you navigate the soul ties and intertwined heart strands you leave behind. I put what matters over my mind to confine the villain in this crime. I pray God delivers you today and everyday what I had for you on my plate.

This was a lot of writing for it not to be a love thing. This book was an open letter and while all the pain was unintentional. I still died and remember being petrified of losing the greatest feeling and you in whom I confided my deepest darkest fears. You can have many but a heart may choose to only love one. That's the lesson for my future son and while it may be more it isn't four because only a few will stick out causing uproars to your central nervous system. I just gave gospel I wonder will you ever listen. The lies you spoke ensured our eyes won't honestly cross paths. Unless a lie is told in advance to avoid that crash. See, I know your biggest secret and that's something I share with your best of friends. You tell a true tale with your own lens. Risking losing everything and everyone even your own kin. I'll never say a bad thing about you but it sounds like full sin. It makes real life experiences feel like pretend. Nothing I'm writing exonerates my hesitation. I just can't get over how you brought things to an end. Like you I just put it in a text. I assure you from the bottom of my heart from the day you first opened your mouth you were going to win.

It's just if you would have told your friends and family the truth. I am certain I'd be sitting here right now with you playing with my young you. That may be appalling to you now but in that moment, it was our truth. I would have still written this book describing our roots.

-Thing 1

Denying The Anger [&] Bargaining With The Truth

I understand you not wanting to face me.

I hurt you broke your heart and untucked the dreams
Unbuckled the life that you gleaned

planted in a pot of change to grow only in sun

It wasn't prepared for clouds and rain
You know doubt, questioning, distrust—games

I fought for you in a summer shower
I never even got close to being wet
Trying to get home to you drenched in sorrow
Soaked in upset

I swam through lies paddled in hate
I ran through why's waded in eyes unable to relate

I tried to hurdle the turtle of time inevitability and fate
You ran out of love as I ran into hate
Revolving door into the store of poor communication
If I ran into you today your face wouldn't state

The nature of or any mistake's
You'd avoid eye contact and agree to save the date
set the truth down to remove a few plates.
That's heavy for you too much weight.

-lies take too much exercise

Charles Stokes

Will someone grab the dust pan?
That broom this mop...
I don't care use hands
Just pick the rest of me up

I've done so much but I need those pieces
My heart
These thoughts
I just need a little help
Picking all this up

A dash of trust
A sprinkle of love
Six or seven hugs
And you'll see

Angel sweetheart knightly
Becomes me
I love I cherish I stay I fight
Please
End this memory for this night
Pick me up
end this chapter of my life

Index

14 Lines of Doubt	63
A Drink	77
Always Gone	19
Angel Eyes	29
An Uneasy Apology	73
At First Sight	36
Bargaining With My Denial	3
Beautiful Mind Soft Hearts	74
Beauty of Life	39
Dear	93
Deep Sea	9
Dreaming	76
Driving Shots	9
DUI	11
Embrace it	35
Epic	83-90
Fall	42
Feeling	59
Fight For you	21
Fighting	91
Friends	30
Grinding My Teeth	81

Haiku	22
I am an ex	7
I'm Alone	15
I'm Over It	79
In a Sentence	4
I Page	53
It's Been Three Long Hard Years, and I Still Love You	60
I Was in Love Once	64-72
I Love This Woman	20
Keep Dreaming	80
Letter to A Friend	55
Let Love Free	41
Lies Take Too Much Exercise	95
Life	8
Lost in it All	47
Love	5
Love Comes in a Spectrum	38
Missing	58
My Love Travels Where Your Wind Blows	24
My Toxic Sugar	40
Near Mars	43
Oblivious	37
Pain	44
Platform	46
Quote	23,28
Red Roses Actually Turn Blue	48
R.E.S.I.S.T	49
Rich and Worthless	76
Sapiosexual	18
Savoir	34

Shattered	16
She Chose Her Fate	10
Spiteful	62
Summer is Disrespectful	61
Tantrum	52
The Truth	51
This Book	2
Three Year Old Road Kill	53
To my Tears	57
Too Much Pride to Crash Your Home Coming	33
Title Bout	82
T'was You Who Labeled me a Stalker	32
Two Hand Touch	14
Untitled	109
You Reap	17
Your Death Killed Me	54
Your Face	50
You Spoke Lies to Life	12

More content can be found at:

www.lovepainandpoetry.com

You can connect with the author and support his cause to combat and de-stigmatize mental health issues by engaging on the website and social media.

Facebook	@lovepainpoetry	
Instagram	@lovepainpoetry	
Twitter	@lovepainpoetry	

"I don't desire to read or hear a Shakespearean Sonnet. I don't think many people do. I want you to rip my heart out grind it up for 60 seconds and leave me in deep thought as you walk back to your seat."

-Short and Sweet

I really hope you enjoyed this book! I hope you love the mix of free verse and prose. I hope you grabbed the concept of poetry, what it is, how to write it or in the case of technically correct poets "RIGHT" poetry. What I gave you isn't enough to be an expert. It will get you started. But come to lovepainandpoetry.com and you will find more detailed instruction in the poetry section. We are constantly seeking new content and poets to contribute.

If you loved the book follow me at the social media provided earlier in the book. If you're reading this it means book two of the series is being completed.

Bye for now.

ABOUT THE AUTHOR

Charles Stokes is an avid writer and veteran from Baltimore, MD. He fought for his country serving in Iraq and Afghanistan. As a writer, Charles finds inspiration from personal experiences. His time at war and his interactions with others throughout his life have given him a deeper understanding of the human experience.

He began writing poetry in 2004 as a hobby and something to pass the time. Charles was reminded of the origins of his poetic journey by his younger brother discovered recorded poems by Charles. His family solidified his commitment to writing poetry with their love and support. The support of his family was a major factor in his decision to continue writing.

Charles recalls the many steps of his journey as a poet. In 2009 he wrote to impress a young woman he admired. Love is a great motivation. There is something profound about committing one's emotions to paper. It's as though one's affections become immortalized

He began to write more frequently while deployed to Afghanistan where he picked up the pen name "Short and Sweet" from someone in an open mic audience. Most of his work fits the pen name due to the concise and provocative nature of his storytelling. His work is very direct and modern. A true understanding of his work can be had when one understands the depth of layers in his poems. His writing style is layered and precise with a touch of the dreamer he never realized he had inside.

In his free time he is a car enthusiast, appreciates sports, and target shooting.

Hawaii is his spiritual home where he feels most at peace. You'll find his work a refreshing read or a great listen. He doesn't consider himself a poet. For Charles, writing is just putting emotion to paper. Writing is the essence of all that is. The life of a poet is merely a journey to capture all that is beautiful about life. Life is poetry in motion and we are all students of the great unknown.

www.ingramcontent.com/pod-product-compliance
Lightning Source LLC
Chambersburg PA
CBHW071214070526
44584CB00019B/3023